SMOKEY JOE GOES TO THE VET

by

KAREN NORDSTROM DUGAN
ILLUSTRATED BY MARY GRACE CORPUS

IndieOwlPressKids

4700 Millenia Blvd
Ste 175 #90776
Orlando, FL 32839

info@indieowlpress.com
IndieOwlPress.com

This book is a work of fiction. Names, characters, places, and incidents are either the product of the author's imagination or are used fictitiously, and any resemblance to actual persons, living or dead, business establishments, events, or locales is entirely coincidental.

Smokey Joe Goes to the Vet

Copyright © 2022 by Karen Nordstrom Dugan

All rights reserved.
No part of this book may be reproduced in any manner without the express written consent of the author, except in the case of brief excerpts in reviews and articles.

Illustrated by Mary Grace Corpus
www.MaryGraceCorpus.com

Edited by Vanessa Anderson at NightOwlFreelance.com

Cover design & Interior layout/design by Vanessa Anderson
Cover art © Mary Grace Corpus

Paperback ISBN: 978-1-949193-17-6
Hardcover ISBN: 978-1-949193-19-0

Printed in the U.S.A.

To my husband Bernie, "da bear."
Our life together has been packed full of adventures.
Building traps to catch stubborn feral cats after caring for their kittens, plucking dead birds from busy highways so I could bury them. (Don't forget the dead shore bird who road home on top of the car.) And, "oh honey, let's just go look at that foster dog!" I could go on and on, but I want you to know that every adventure has deepened my love for you more than you'll ever know. You'll always be my hero, my rescuer, my best friend, and the man every woman dreams of marrying. Until the twelfth of never...
— K

"Cats don't like change without their consent."
— Roger Caras

SMOKEY JOE GOES TO THE VET

The poplars and oaks have shed their leaves along the tree lined road. The red sumacs are bare but standing tall. Neighbors walk their fur babies with jackets on but still take time to stop and talk about their care. Even the stroller baby who's wheeled from place to place seems content within its quilted covered fortress, sitting impatiently waiting for conversations to end.

When will they let me out to pee? she thinks to herself. Then wiggles with delight when she's lifted to freedom.

Two legged's who care for their furry friends seem to enjoy a routine that also allows for time to meet their neighbors and catch up on the daily gossip.

Those who rescue abandoned animals have a different routine. They must first see to the animal's health and tend to any issues resulting from the fur babies years of living a hobo's life.

The hobo's life is one of finding shelter against the rain and snow. They must be aware of busy streets, other animals aimed at making them their evening meal, and finding food to eat that is usually much less desirable than their cared-for counterparts. Such was the case with Smokey Joe.

With quiet nervousness, Smokey Joe was brought inside the ivory house by the kind lady. The scents he was used to were gone.

My fortress where I can watch and wait is now out of reach, he thought. *Captivity is a two-way street,* he pondered as he looked around the strange room filled with unfamiliar surroundings.

The lady gently placed him on a warm blanket and showed him new things to consider. Then she quietly whispered, "You get some rest, Smokey Joe, I'll be back in a short while. You're safe now," and she left him to investigate his surroundings.

Inside the house, time passed differently for Smokey Joe than it had in the past. It seemed to move slower and carried a sense of peace that he eventually found soothing.

There were noises from inside the ivory house that permeated his sleepiness. Every sound was new. Usually, two legged's talking together. Also, a sound like rushing water would always startle him: it was coming from two different areas. Doors opening and closing. And a melodic sound that frequently changed pace and tone seemed to emanate from a noisy box right next to the room in which he huddled.

His gray ears perked while listening to sounds like popular candy bar commercials. His favorite was the one with the word "Kat" in it. There were also sounds that caused Smokey Joe to pause with concern and wonder, *where IS the valley of the jolly green giant? And where in this room could I hide if that guy ever showed up?* There was one commercial he particularly liked. He would wake from his cat nap, stretch, and perk his ears whenever he heard it. "Meow...meow...meow... meow" it said...about a cat food often "requested by name." *I could listen to that one all day!* he thought.

All in all, it wasn't a difficult transition to make, especially when the lady would come in four times a day and bring him the most scrumptious food! There were fish treats and chicken, beef and tuna. Dry morsels were beginning to clean his teeth, and his favorite were the small licks of lactose-free milk once in a while. It would bring back a faint memory of his kitten days, and a warm feeling would envelope him.

He began to look forward to the lady's visits, and he liked the soft and reassuring way she spoke. She had a comforting way of cooing to him as she stroked his fur. These were the moments he loved best. She would pull off those nasty black things that caused him to bite himself as his chortled purrs would rise and fall in tones he'd never heard before. *YES!! This is a life! My wily hobo friends could never dream this up!* he thought.

The days passed slowly as he settled in and adjusted to each routine. One change that made him shrink with concern was the day the lady brought in a small box. She placed it on the floor, slowly opening its wire door for his inspection, and left him to investigate. *Now what am I to do with this?* he mumbled to himself. *This will take some major investigation!*

Approaching slowly, paws stretched to their limits, he sniffed and sniffed this strange box and wondered what it was for. *Hope I'm not going in there,* he worried. The box sat in the middle of the room for most of the morning, causing Smokey Joe to miss a much-needed nap as he kept a weary-eye fixated on it.

Soon, the lady came in and quietly picked him up.

Yep! I'm going in, he snarled as she contorted his body and gently guided him in. The inside was lined with a woolen mat that felt rather inviting, so, with mild hesitation—and no room to protest—he laid down.

Now, most wily street cats have no idea what a vehicle is, aside from their warmth in winter time, but one roar of the engine and a jolt forward quickly showed him their purpose. The trees passed quickly, so many of them, as he peered from the grated door. *I knew this life was too good to be true,* he thought. *I hope there's food at the next place!*

Soon he was carried through a big door, and the smells almost overtook him. *Fur and chemicals, ringing phones, and much more noise than the ivory house.* He shuddered. *What was that? What did he hear the lady say? Somebody better tell me what a vet is, and pretty quick!* he snarled inside.

Suddenly, the box seemed the safest place to be! *Uh oh... I'm doomed,* he thought, sinking deeper into the wool mat. *Should have never trusted two legged's!* he mused. Quivering, he wondered how he would ever survive the fear that was growing inside. Before long, gentle arms reached into the box and pulled him to a warm coat with a gentle heart beating inside.

"Hang in there, fella, we'll be back home before you know it. It's just a checkup to see that you're alright," she cooed in his ear, holding him close. "You'll meet some wonderful people here."

Just for a second, his quivering body relaxed, but then the door swung open and a lady in a white coat walked in. "So who do we have here?" she said.

"Meet Smokey Joe," the lady from the ivory tower replied. He needs a health checkup. He's been living a hobo's life for quite a while, and I want to be sure he's healthy.

Taking him from his lady's arms caused some mild distress, as this person called "vet" inspected his whole body.

Yeow–watch it, lady, that's my ears. Yikes! And those are my arms and legs–they work just fine! he snapped. Yea, yea, and my fur's just fine too. I bathed this morning! he cursed.

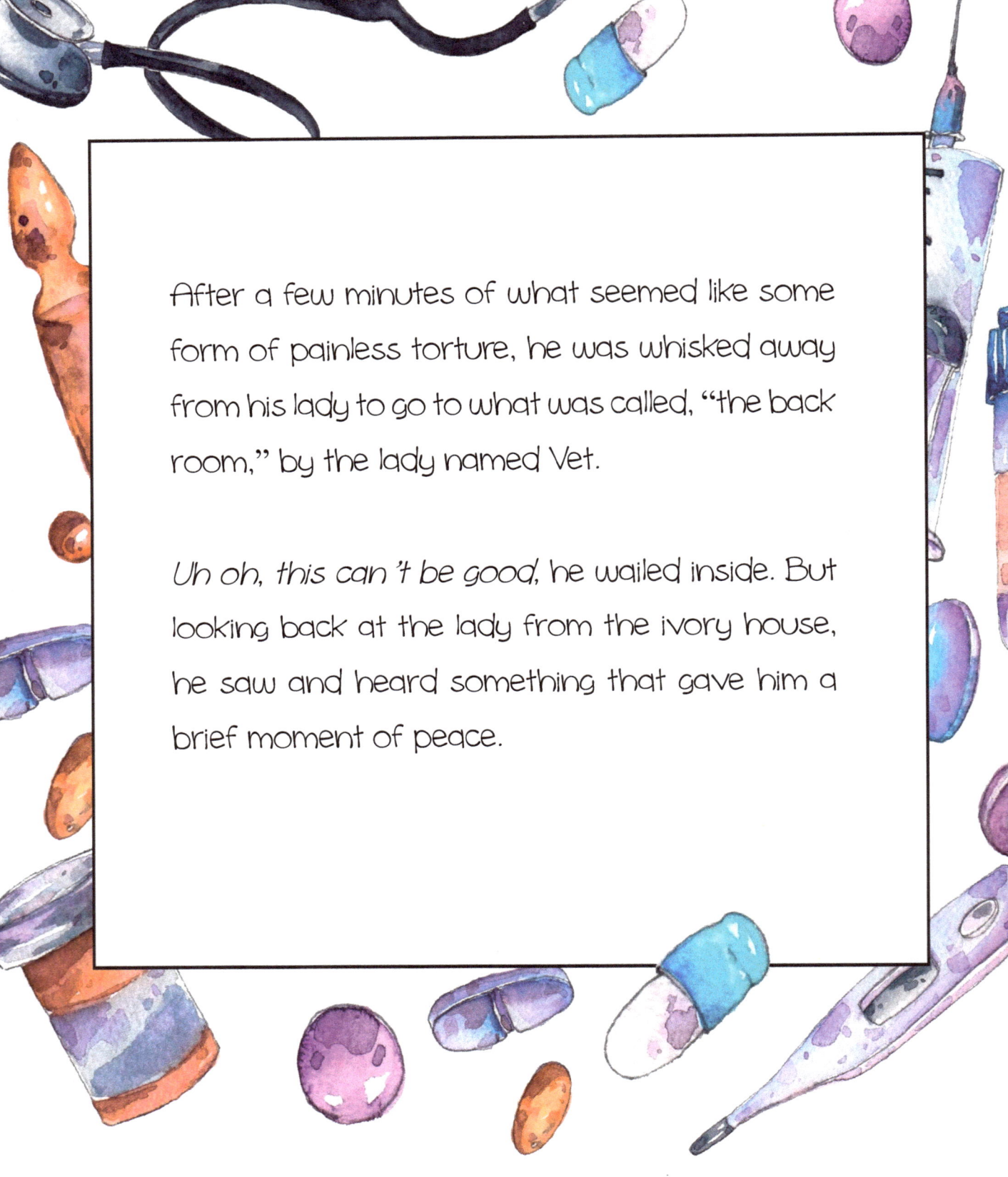

After a few minutes of what seemed like some form of painless torture, he was whisked away from his lady to go to what was called, "the back room," by the lady named Vet.

Uh oh, this can't be good, he wailed inside. But looking back at the lady from the ivory house, he saw and heard something that gave him a brief moment of peace.

With a smile on her face, and a soft reassuring voice, she said, "You'll be back soon, Smokey Joe, and I'll be waiting here for you, then we'll go home."

All four legged's must dread what they're going to find when they're whisked away from their comfort zone to go *in the back* at the Vet. Smokey Joe was no different. His new world had just shifted into noises and smells that went beyond his understanding.

He even pondered a very strange sight as he looked out the window: a small dog, much like the one's he used to watch from his green fortress, was being followed across the lawn outside by a lady with a long stick with a bowl on the end. Every time the poor dog lifted his leg, she was poking it under him. *What kind of torture palace was he in?* he howled inside.

Now it's my turn. *Yeow...what was that...and why did she put it there!? Oh, I'm not going to stand for this,* he snarled inside. *Why'd she put that around my paw?...*And soon after, a pinch that reminded him of those pesky yellow buzzers that used to fly around and plague him every time he napped where the dandelions grew. *I hate this place, put me back in the box!* he howled.

Children soon learn that doctor visits are necessary and only a brief change in their routine. Our animal friends act no differently when it's time to go to the doctor for a checkup.

Smokey Joe was learning to trust and have courage when faced with new experiences because he remembered the comfort and attention he'd experienced from his lady waiting in the next room...*but I don't have to like it!* he decided as he licked at the pinch on his paw.

Before long, Smokey's newfound courage paid off. He was soon back in the safety of his warm box and those same trees were once again whizzing by outside.

Returning home, his lady gently sat his box down, opened the door, and left the room.

Nooooo thank you, I'll stay in here if you don't mind, he thought as he nestled deeper into its soft surface. The sun had shifted across the windows before he felt safe enough to venture from his box.

His lady seemed occupied, looking up information on the small device in her hand. Those meaty morsels she'd placed before him helped a lot, but something was different.

His lady was quiet as she sat on the floor next to him while he ate. She stroked him softly as his familiar chortle began easing from his throat. When he turned to gaze at her, her face was shadowed in sadness, and tears fell from her eyes. *Why is my lady sad,* he pondered. *What could it be, and where do we go from here?* he thought with a quick pause, looking deeply into her eyes, he blinked briefly and rubbed his head on her outstretched hand.

He remembered how lonely his days used to be and quickly focused on the wonderful meal just put before him. But being a tried 'n' true live-in-the-moment hobo, he thought about how *tomorrow will have to wait* and quietly returned to his meal.

Time passed before his lady slowly left him to settle in for a much-needed nap on his mat by the window. Animals can quickly sense energy changes in humans, and whatever was different in his lady concerned him a little, but not enough to keep him from a much needed nap after a very tiring day.

Author's Note

My observations through the years are that cats hate change, but adults and children can learn how to help any pet cope with their vet visits. Remaining calm themselves is the key because animals can sense dread from their humans.

1. Make their carrier a cozy place to snack and nap in before the visit.
2. Take short trips in the car that aren't related to a vet visit.
3. Cover your kitty carrier with something with the scent from home to help soothe them in a busy vet's waiting room.
4. Use a soothing voice, and have their favorite treats on hand.

If you're as lucky as Smokey Joe was, you'll already have a caring and wonderful vet with a kind staff, who know how to respond to your pet's fear. This is the message in Smokey Joe goes to the Vet.

A portion of all book sales will be donated to:
www.aspca.org
www.abandonedpetproject.org

Further Reading

The Mystery of Smokey Joe

Forthcoming

Smokey Joe Goes to Heaven

SPECIAL THANKS TO THE ANGELS AT NEWBERRY ANIMAL HEALTH CARE CENTER

L-R: Lia, Dr. Angela Neubaum, Amanda, Jessica, Abby

About the Author

Karen Nordstrom Dugan has studied animal communication, and she works tirelessly rescuing and finding homes for abandoned and unwanted animals. She enjoys history, writing, travel, and is currently writing about her 82nd-Airborne Uncle and the recovery of soldiers missing in action from WWII. She has five adult children, and four grandchildren. She lives near Harrisburg, Pa with her husband, Bernie, and several spoiled fur babies.

www.ingramcontent.com/pod-product-compliance
Lightning Source LLC
Chambersburg PA
CBHW041236240426
43673CB00011B/354